Put Beginning Readers on the Right Track with
ALL ABOARD READING™

The All Aboard Reading series is especially designed for beginning readers. Written by noted authors and illustrated in full color, these are books that children really want to read—books to excite their imagination, expand their interests, make them laugh, and support their feelings. With fiction and nonfiction stories that are high interest and curriculum-related, All Aboard Reading books offer something for every young reader. And with four different reading levels, the All Aboard Reading series lets you choose which books are most appropriate for your children and their growing abilities.

Picture Readers
Picture Readers have super-simple texts, with many nouns appearing as rebus pictures. At the end of each book are 24 flash cards—on one side is a rebus picture; on the other side is the written-out word.

Station Stop 1
Station Stop 1 books are best for children who have just begun to read. Simple words and big type make these early reading experiences more comfortable. Picture clues help children to figure out the words on the page. Lots of repetition throughout the text helps children to predict the next word or phrase—an essential step in developing word recognition.

Station Stop 2
Station Stop 2 books are written specifically for children who are reading with help. Short sentences make it easier for early readers to understand what they are reading. Simple plots and simple dialogue help children with reading comprehension.

Station Stop 3
Station Stop 3 books are perfect for children who are reading alone. With longer text and harder words, these books appeal to children who have mastered basic reading skills. More complex stories captivate children who are ready for more challenging books.

In addition to All Aboard Reading books, look for All Aboard Math Readers™ (fiction stories that teach math concepts children are learning in school); All Aboard Science Readers™ (nonfiction books that explore the most fascinating science topics in age-appropriate language); All Aboard Poetry Readers™ (funny, rhyming poems for readers of all levels); and All Aboard Mystery Readers™ (puzzling tales where children piece together evidence with the characters).

All Aboard for happy reading!

For Bob—C.S.

GROSSET & DUNLAP
Published by the Penguin Group
Penguin Group (USA) Inc., 375 Hudson Street, New York, New York 10014, U.S.A.
Penguin Group (Canada), 90 Eglinton Avenue East, Suite 700, Toronto, Ontario, Canada M4P
2Y3 (a division of Pearson Penguin Canada Inc.)
Penguin Books Ltd, 80 Strand, London WC2R 0RL, England
Penguin Ireland, 25 St Stephen's Green, Dublin 2, Ireland
(a division of Penguin Books Ltd)
Penguin Group (Australia), 250 Camberwell Road, Camberwell, Victoria 3124, Australia
(a division of Pearson Australia Group Pty Ltd)
Penguin Books India Pvt Ltd, 11 Community Centre,
Panchsheel Park, New Delhi - 110 017, India
Penguin Group (NZ), 67 Apollo Drive, Mairangi Bay, Auckland 1311, New Zealand
(a division of Pearson New Zealand Ltd.)
Penguin Books (South Africa) (Pty) Ltd, 24 Sturdee Avenue,
Rosebank, Johannesburg 2196, South Africa

Penguin Books Ltd, Registered Offices:
80 Strand, London WC2R 0RL, England

Library of Congress Cataloging-in-Publication Data

Edwards, Roberta.
Emperor penguins / by Roberta Edwards ; illustrated by Carol Schwartz.
p. cm. — (All aboard science reader. Station stop 2)
ISBN 978-0-448-44664-6 (pbk.)
1. Emperor penguin—Juvenile literature. I. Schwartz, Carol, 1954– ill. II. Title.
QL696.S473E39 2007
598.47—dc22
2007000463

10 9 8 7 6 5 4 3 2 1

Emperor Penguins

By Roberta Edwards
Illustrated by Carol Schwartz

Grosset & Dunlap

A penguin is not your average bird.

Why?

Well, for one thing,

penguins can't fly.

They can't even flutter off the ground.

Their wings are more like flippers.

And that's a good thing.

Because penguins like to swim.

Ducks paddle, and swans glide.

But penguins zoom underwater.

Some can go 25 miles an hour.

That's faster than any other bird.

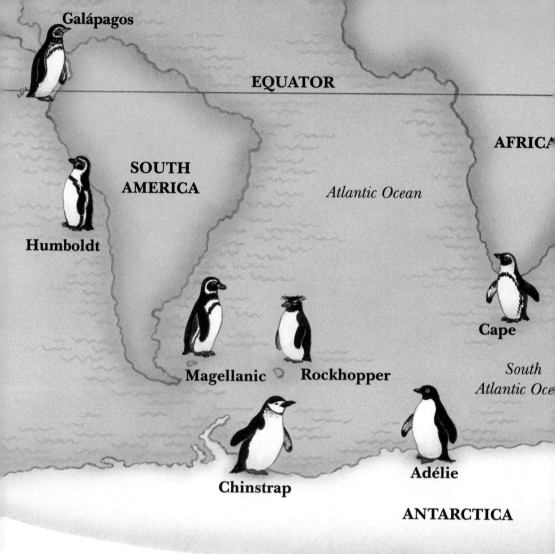

Galápagos

EQUATOR

AFRICA

SOUTH
AMERICA

Atlantic Ocean

Humboldt

Cape

Magellanic   Rockhopper

South
Atlantic Oce

Chinstrap

Adélie

ANTARCTICA

There are many different kinds
of penguins.

Indian Ocean

AUSTRALIA

Snares crested

Macaroni

Fairy

Emperor

King

Gentoo

Yellow-eyed

All—except the Galápagos penguin—
live south of the equator.
The map shows you where.

Rockhopper penguins have
funny plumes
on their heads.

Fairy penguins are the smallest.

They grow to be only

about 16 inches tall.

The largest penguin is

the emperor penguin.

It stands almost four feet high.

It lives in Antarctica.

No people live in Antarctica.
Only a few animals live there—
seals and killer whales and
certain birds of prey.
For all other creatures
it is too cold.
There are no trees
or grass or flowers.

Just ice, ice, and more ice.

In summer it can be

30 degrees below zero.

In winter, the temperature may drop

to 80 degrees below zero.

Winds can whip up to

100 miles an hour.

Winters are harsher than
anywhere else on Earth.
Yet Antarctica is home to about
40 groups of penguins.
Each group is called a "colony."
A colony may have as many as
40,000 penguins in it.
How can emperor penguins
survive the cold?
The fat in their bodies
helps keep them warm.
So does their thick, short coat
of feathers.

On land

emperor penguins waddle

on their strong, webbed feet.

They hop and use their beaks and claws
to go up hills.
Then they flop on their bellies and . . .

Whoosh!

Down the hill they go.

It's like sledding.

The water is ice-cold, too.

But this is where they are most at home.

They can stay underwater

for almost 20 minutes.

They can dive way down deep.

In fact, some emperor penguins

can dive 900 feet below

the water's surface.

In the inky black water,
they hunt for fish and squid.

Like all penguins,

emperor penguins have

black backs

and white bellies.

These colors help protect them

from enemies.

In the water,

leopard seals and killer whales

hunt for emperor penguins.

From below

the penguin's white belly

blends in

with the ice.

It's hard for enemies

to see them.

Large birds like petrels

also hunt for emperor penguins.

But from above

the penguin's black back

blends in with the dark water.

Still, a petrel may spot a penguin.

Then it will swoop down.

The penguin has to swim away fast!

Like all birds,
emperor penguins lay eggs.
In March they go inland
to their nesting grounds.
That is the place where
they were all born.

But they do not build nests

for their eggs.

There are no twigs or grass around.

In May, the egg is laid.

The mother penguin is very hungry now.

She wants to hunt for fish.

She passes the egg to her mate.

She must do it very, very carefully—

or else the egg can crack.

How does the egg stay safe
in such cold weather?
The male penguin tucks the egg
under a flap on his belly.
(This flap is called a "brood pouch.")
The egg rests on his feet.
Now it is safe and warm.

The mother penguins
begin a long walk to the sea.
There, they will feast on fish
and krill and squid.

It will be two months before
the mother penguins return
to their eggs.

For those two months

the father penguins

keep holding the egg.

During this time

the weather gets much colder.

Storms come.

The male penguins huddle together.

They take turns

being in the middle.

It is warmest there.

At last the mother penguins return.

It is now July.

The penguins find their mate
by calling to each other.

They know their mate's sound.

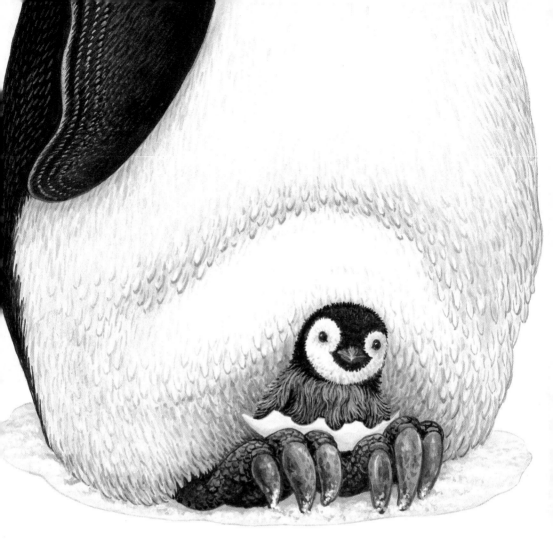

Many chicks have just hatched.

They are less than a pound.

They are covered in fuzz.

They make soft peeps.

Right away,

the male penguin passes the chick

to the female.

The fathers have not eaten

in months.

Now it is their turn

to feast in the sea.

At first the chicks stay very close
to their mother.
They get their food from
inside their mother's throat.
The little chicks grow quickly.

At last

the male penguins return.

The chicks peep and squeak.

It is as if they are calling,

"Here I am! Here I am!"

In this way,

the male penguin finds his family.

For a little while

all three penguins spend time together.

The chicks get bigger.

They grow downy feathers.

But they are gray,

not black and white.

They spend more time

with other penguin chicks.

The days grow longer.

By December

the chicks are ready to live on their own.

They have their grown-up feathers.

They begin their first trip

to the sea.

Nobody teaches them to swim.

All on their own, they know how.

They will hunt and play in the water.

They will try to stay away from enemies.

For four years

they will live in the sea

and at the water's edge.

Then they will travel the long miles

to the nesting grounds.

And one day in June,

can you guess what will happen?

An egg will hatch
and—*peep, peep, peep!*—
out will come a little chick.
It will look around
and see ice, ice, and more ice.
This is home
to the emperor penguins.